Quakerism in the 21st Century

Philip Rack

William Sessions Limited
York, England

ISBN 1 85072 279 X

ACKNOWLEDGEMENTS

I am grateful to the following Friends and friends who read the manuscript in various stages of preparation, and made suggestions, some of which I have followed.

Gill Boocock; Donald Bush; Adam Curle; Robert Gibson; Lois & David Jenkins; Eva Pinthus; Jennifer Rack; Tony Smith; and Alex Tindall.

The views expressed here, however, and any errors of fact or interpretation, are entirely my own responsibility.

Printed in 11 on 12 point Plantin Typeface
from Author's Disk
by Sessions of York
The Ebor Press
York, England

Contents

Foreword

THIS PERSONAL HISTORY gives an account of developments in the Religious Society of Friends during the life-time of the author but including major events back to the very beginnings of the Society.

There is much to interest most readers as the changes in attitudes among the members of the Society to theological and social problems are described in Chapter 1. When the author was growing up views about Christ, God, Christianity, prayer, and Quaker theory and practice were all as avidly discussed as they are now but the conclusions reached were not the same as those of today. What are we to make of this? Do the meanings of the doctrines change with the generations?

In chapter 2, in an ecumenical context, we are confronted by the value of Quaker connections with non-church groups such as Greenpeace, Amnesty International, CND and so forth. The place of ecumenism is put into its rightful perspective, the doctrines of church Christianity are subject to trenchant evaluation, but "good works" are approved, whether done by Christians or not.

The next chapter begins with a look at the foundation and early history of the Society, which leads on to our mode of decision-taking and the writing of minutes. This is followed by a discussion about our susceptibility to hierarchy in the Society. It is suggested that this tendency is countered by the devotion to service in the world, for which Quakers are recognised, if for nothing else.

This theme is continued in Chapter 4, but here the emphasis is more on Meeting for Worship. Here the author writes, "I think that among British Friends today the most significant division is not between so-called Universalist and Christocentric tendencies, but between those who have experienced the reality of a gathered meeting and those who have not, or have forgotten it". This chapter is concerned with a topic of major importance, because there is no doubt that the Society suffers at present from a good deal of ill-informed and prejudiced debate about it.

In the final chapter the need for a wider circle of friends of Friends is advocated even if such friends do not conform to the usual pattern of Quakers. This challenge is illustrated by postulating what might happen if outreach actually worked and brought in some rather rougher types than we are used to, some who expected action as well as talk. Heaven forfend!

In summary, for anyone who wishes to read a review of some of the important questions which have arisen in the Society, especially in the last 100 years, this would be a very good place to start. It will help both new attenders and members and it will remind established Quakers what their Society stands for.

Alex Tindall
Editor, Quaker Forum

1

THE SOCIETY OF Friends in Britain is changing. Several recent Swarthmore lecturers and contributors to The Friend have emphasised that. Many Friends view with misgivings the changes they perceive. More than one has said in my hearing: *"This is not the Society I joined"*, with the implicit rider: *"Do I still belong here?"*. That is sad. On the other hand there are others who would like our Society to change more, or faster, than it is doing. There is sadness there, too.

Let me admit straight away that I belong in the second group. I would like to see more change. In recent years I have come to regard some of our traditional Quaker habits of thought and expression as outmoded and stultifying. I would like us to make a big effort to escape from them. I know there are quite a few in the Society who share that view. More seriously, I believe those defects have caused several former members to lose heart and leave. More seriously still, I suspect they have deterred an even greater number who might have joined us.

These are not trivial issues. One cannot hope to write about them without being contentious, and risk causing pain. I apologise in advance for that. Perhaps it may help if, before suggesting where I think we should be going, I say where I think we are coming from.

I have been a Friend for 70 years. Let me try to describe the beliefs and practices of the Friends among whom I grew up. My family were part of a small group in north Lincolnshire. They started the North Lincolnshire "Allowed" Meeting, (it would now be called a "Recognised" meeting"), which later gave birth to Preparative Meetings at Grimsby and Scunthorpe. In the early days there were four or five families involved, spread over a large rural area.

1

My ancestors were not Quakers. My parents joined the Society shortly before I was born. They were each brought up in Methodist households in northern industrial cities, in environments which at the end of the 19th century were harsh. Both escaped from their backgrounds, and left their Methodism behind with the rest of their working-class culture. As young adults their loyalties lay with the Holiday Fellowship and, later, the Left Book Club. But in the 1920's they somehow became aware of the Society of Friends. They wrote to Friends House. The reply came that the nearest Meeting was at Lincoln, 40 miles away – a long way to travel in those days. Then came a second message from Friends House. There was a Friend, travelling in the Ministry, who would divert his journey to visit them, if they would accommodate him overnight. So it was arranged. In due course my father waited to meet the visitor at our local railway station. Many years later he described the scene to me.

An elderly man approached the ticket barrier, and was heard to say to the ticket collector:

"I have travelled from Doncaster. As you see, I have a Third Class ticket. Unfortunately there were no Third Class seats available, so I was obliged to occupy a First Class compartment. Will you tell me, therefore, please, how much I owe you?"

I don't know what the ticket collector made of that! The visitor was Neave Brayshaw. My father took him home, and no doubt there were discussions long into the night. Whatever was said it was the scene at the ticket barrier that stuck in my parents' minds.

My first attendances at meeting were in a cradle. As a small child I remember Sunday Meetings held in our and other people's sitting rooms. I also remember Monthly Meetings at Lincoln and further afield, whole-day outings made more acceptable to me because before the war, and even during it, Lincolnshire Friends could produce a magnificent Monthly Meeting Tea, and there were large motherly ladies who loved to indulge a small boy. And at older meeting houses such as Brant Broughton there were musty, dusty galleries smelling of pitchpine and hassocks, and old farm buildings and lofts full of hay on the Burtt family's farm.

I spent ten years as a pupil at Quaker Schools, Ackworth first and then Bootham, coming under the influence of such teachers as Arthur Cooper, Philip Radley, Tom Green, and visiting worthies like Jack Hoyland, Hugh Doncaster, Elfrida Vipont Foulds, Reginald Reynolds and Kenneth Barnes. At one time I would have denied that they had any lasting influence: but now I know better.

After school my Quakerly career continued at Jesus Lane Meeting in Cambridge and the tutelage of such Friends as Anna Bidder, Hilda Sturge, Damaris Parker-Rhodes, and the fellowship of Cambridge Young Friends, where I had my first experience of clerking, and we had the privilege of meeting many notable Friends, among them George Gorman and Duncan Fairn, to name but two. The war was over, but National Service was still in force, so every male Young Friend was faced at the age of 18 with the choice – to join the armed forces, or be a conscientious objector, and that requirement certainly made us clarify our thoughts and beliefs. Those who chose to "join up" were never (as far as I know) criticised by Friends. Khaki uniforms were occasionally seen in meeting, without comment. I think it was assumed that each was following the path that seemed to him to be right for him. For those who chose to be "C.O's" the usual form of alternative service was the Friends Relief Service, and that was an important formative influence for many. So, too, were Work Camps where we found fellowship and mutual support.

In 1963, John Robinson, then Bishop of Woolwich, published his famous paperback "Honest to God".[1] It had a tremendous impact on "believers" and "non-believers" alike. It seemed to offer a theology that non-theologians could understand and discuss in straightforward language. A few years later Home Service Committee published a booklet by a group of Friends, called "Towards a Quaker View of Sex". This contained ideas about homosexuality and extramarital sex which were radical for the time. They were a breath of fresh air to members of my generation, but scandalised many older Friends.

Those were some of the influences in my youth. What did those Quakers believe? How did they behave?

They were not, I think, what is now called "Christ-centred". God-centred, perhaps. They might not necessarily have tried hard to define what they meant by God, but He – (or in those days possibly "It", but never "She") – was a reality to them and a source of guidance and inspiration. To some, no doubt, God was the *Holy, hidden Being* we sang about. For others the image may have been more abstract; but probably all could unite in the verse: *"How shall we love thee .... if we love not the world which thou hast made?"* Ideas like "God is a process" or "God is not a noun but a verb" were not around at the time. I think such ideas would have been startling to the weighty Friends of my youth, but some at least would have been prepared to give them consideration.

Knowledge of the Bible was displayed naturally by adult Friends, and was taught to the young, with some judicious editing. The main emphasis was on the New Testament. The Old Testament was quarried by teachers for improving texts, while naughty little boys sniggered about the "rude bits", but it was not accorded the same authority as the New Testament. My recollection is that it was offered much like the Norse or Greek legends – good stories which contained symbolic significance and some useful moral precepts. It also provided glimpses of Hebrew tribal beliefs which were the seedbed of Christianity. We knew the Genesis story as myth, and were never led to suppose it was anything else. (By myth, I mean a story which is not literally true but embodies a truth).

Friends may have been "Christ-centred" in the sense that they regarded the life of Jesus of Nazareth as the most important event that ever took place on earth; but issues of "Incarnation", "Redemption", and "Atonement" as understood in mainstream Christian doctrine, were side-stepped. Even schoolteachers who didn't claim to be expert theologians were sufficiently familiar with biblical research and scholarship to have some scepticism about the accuracy of the written records – a scepticism we were positively encouraged to share. When in later life I encountered people who insisted on the literal truth of the whole bible I found that amazing – and still do. That kind of fundamentalism was never part of the Quakerism of my childhood.

Jesus was clearly a hero figure, head and shoulders above all others and unique. The story of the crucifixion was accepted as one of those archetypal stories that was true and important – even if it didn't actually happen in precisely that way at that exact place and time (and whether it did or not was not worth spending much time on). Statements like; *"You've got to believe everything in the Gospels, Brother, or reject everything.....you can't pick and choose"* – statements beloved of a certain type of evangelist and occasionally heard even today in Quaker ministry – would not have been acceptable to most of the Quakers of my youth.

4

Though Jesus was the primary inspiration, it was inherent in the Quakerism that I am trying to describe that the life of Christ was not the only revelation in the world of God's nature or purpose. Partial revelations had occurred before Christ – what else was the Old Testament about? – and since, including some of the Christian saints. George Fox's statement that "Christ has come to teach his people himself" was taken to mean that the holy spirit overwhelmingly manifested in Jesus, was manifested again, albeit much less brightly, in the lives of Fox and countless other people.

Jesus was a channel to God, and the major channel for members of the human race born in the last two millennia in the parts of the world which we now call Christendom. But he was not the only channel. People who were born earlier, or who never heard of Jesus, could not be damned and doomed because of that accident of birth. That was inconsistent with any notion of a loving creator. Those evangelists who believe that Jesus is "The Only Way", and are so fond of using Capital Letters to say so, had some explaining to do.

Is that the statement of a Universalist? If so, I think the label fitted many Quakers I grew up with. Certainly we were offered role models and moral tracts and fragments of teaching from other faiths. One of the moral heroes of the time in Quaker circles was Mahatma Gandhi. Occasionally well-meaning people would suggest that Gandhi was "really a Christian underneath" or "really a sort of Quaker", but it didn't carry conviction, (though his friendship with Horace Alexander was often mentioned). Other examples were paraded before us of people who were not Christians but apparently possessed a greater amount of "*that of God*" than some of our Christian neighbours. Is this Universalism? And if it is, is it therefore not Christianity? Whether it be Christian or not, I believe that it is inherent in Quakerism. Perhaps this was an example, even then, of Quakerism extending beyond the boundaries of Christianity.

"God-centred", or "Spirit-centred", then, rather than "Christ-centred".* I don't remember any exhortation to: "*...accept the Lord Jesus Christ as your Lord and Saviour*". I still find it difficult to know

---

* For discussion of this distinction see Gerald Richards 1978.[2]

5

what such statements really mean. I think that, for the Friends I am recalling, God was present in Meeting for Worship (at least on good days), but the reference was to God or the Spirit, not to Christ. Perhaps I am overstating this, or drawing on too narrow a range of experience. Maybe there were many to whom the picture "The Presence in the Midst" had real inspirational meaning. Personally, I disliked it then and ever since.

When Quakers prayed they did not conclude with stock phrases such as *"We ask this in Jesus' name"*, or *"Through Jesus Christ our Lord...."* The omission was not accidental or insignificant. Nor did the Quakers I knew conclude a vocal prayer with the word *"Amen"*. I was taught that this is because vocal prayer during meeting is merely a temporary audible expression of what is assumed to be going on silently throughout. Its beginning and end do not need to be marked; and talking to God is (in theory) such a natural and continuing process that there's no need to put on a special voice or adopt a special posture for it; and certainly no need for stereotyped ritual phrases.

Yet I remember that in one meeting (was it Ackworth?) it was the custom that when a Friend stood up to give ministry the rest of us remained seated, except when the ministry took the form of prayer, in which case we all stood up. With hindsight, that seems odd. I don't know what to make of it.

Vocal prayer was quite rare, then as now, in many meetings, and I suspect that a lot of Friends were a bit ill-at-ease about it. Certainly there was little place for the sort of declamatory prayer in which the pray-er takes it upon him- or her-self to address God on behalf of the group – in the style of – *"We, Thy people, humbly beseech you, O Lord......"* Flowery language would be avoided in talking to God just as in other conversations. No need for: *"Almighty God, our Gracious and Heavenly Father,....."* One of our Advices states: "God doesn't need information" He didn't need flattery either!

The recent fashion for addressing the almighty as *"Dear Father/mother God"* would have provoked some unquakerly derision. Any Friend with antisexist sensitivities, if they existed at that time, could have found a simpler way to make the point – probably simply leaving out the word "Father" altogether.

Intercessory prayer seems to come naturally to some Quakers, and also what Anna Bidder used to call the "heavenly shopping list". To me there has always been a problem if the implicit message is: *"God, whatever you were planning to do, if I ask you ever so nicely will you change your mind?"* And as for: *"Let's ask the Lord to find us a parking space"* – well, Quakers expected to find their own parking spaces.

One of the definitions of prayer which emerged from late-night Young Friends discussions, was something like: *"to put oneself in a certain posture in one's relationships with God and one's fellows: a posture which, if we were perfect, we would be able to maintain all the time – but we can't manage that, so we make a special effort at certain times".* Does that come anywhere near describing prayer? Does it describe what happens in Meeting? Is it anywhere near the meaning (one of the meanings) of the word "worship"?

As I remember it, theology as a theoretical discipline was not taken very seriously. We were exhorted to act our beliefs instead of talking about them – to "let our lives speak"; to *"show forth Thy praise not only with our lips but in our lives".* Such texts as *"Laborare est Orare",* or *"Who sweeps a room as for Thy laws makes that and the action fine";* and similar injunctions, took the place of theoretical deliberations. "Quaker Thinkers" were less valued than Quaker do-ers. Polished prose from Friends House or Woodbrooke cut less ice than the practical example of an ordinary local Friend living his or her life with a modicum of decency and Quakerly concern. By their fruits should we know them. *"Not everyone who saith unto me: "Lord, Lord"....but he that doeth the will of my Father....."*

Actually, I don't recall much saying of *"Lord, Lord!"* anyway. Were public parades of piety felt to be a bit pharisaic? Jesus recommended that such folk should take themselves off to a private chamber – better for them and certainly more comfortable for the rest of us. There wasn't much room in my kind of Quakerism for the *"Hallelujah, Praise the Lord"* approach. Any Friend who sat in meeting with hands outstretched and upturned, as if to receive a benison from above, would have been an embarrassment. Mind you, there were always a few embarrassingly eccentric Friends around. I hope we were not too intolerant of them.

We did not pay much attention to the Church calendar. Early Friends had refused to acknowledge the distinctiveness of Sunday, and they kept their shops open on Christmas Day. That extreme purism had been diluted by the time I am describing, but it persisted to some extent. No doubt in Friends households Christmas was celebrated with its religious significance fully recognised, but I do not recall special Christmas Day Meetings for Worship, with or without carols and Christingles. The significance of Easter would be mentioned in ministry, more likely linked with seasonal references to re-birth (lambs and daffodils) than with theological concepts of redemption or atonement. Pentecost usually provoked some relevant ministry. Maybe the image of faithful disciples sitting together in an upper room was one that Friends could recognise: and perhaps there was the hope that sometime our Meeting, too, might be blessed by an outpouring of the Spirit. We didn't pay much attention to Lent, or Advent, or the other festivals. They were not part of Quakerism.

At the schools, Meetings for Worship were based on silence, but we also sang hymns, and had readings, and short addresses from members of staff or visiting Friends. I'm glad we did. Quite a lot of it has stuck in my mind, to my benefit. But I remember thinking that the "pure" form of Quaker worship was silence, broken only by occasional spontaneous ministry; and deviations from the pure form were a concession for children who couldn't cope with a full measure of the "real thing". I think that feeling lingers on in me and has given me a rather snobbish attitude to Programmed Meetings. Even at an early age I was very dubious about some of the sentiments expressed in hymns. Singing hymns was enjoyable, Handel's Messiah or Bach's Matthew Passion even more so, but it was important not to get carried away. I think the fear of being "carried away" must have been inculcated in me at a very early age. Maybe it was because I was born into a particularly inhibited family, but I associate it also with Quakerism. I've always had a strong distaste for the use of procedures designed to induce religious fervour, and that distaste has been reinforced by my adult experiences in psychology and psychiatry. Other denominations may use sensory stimuli and emotion-inducing techniques routinely – incense, incantation, Hell-fire imagery, or group pressure to *"Come to the front and give yourself to the Lord"*. Quakers don't do things like that.

They used to, of course. From George Fox's Journal it's quite clear that early meetings were often highly emotionally charged affairs, in which people were "broken" and "brought into the Light" with great dramatic effect and loss of self-control. But in recent centuries in this country that's not been the case – and personally I wouldn't want it back. Obviously not all modern Friends agree: some seem to find singing and handclapping and a degree of Hallelujah-hullabaloo quite acceptable. I suggest they read Will Sargent's classic *"Battle for the Mind"*.[3]

About the Arts, Quakers in my youth were ambivalent. Appreciation of art was not discouraged as it had been earlier, and music played a part in school worship; but as far as I recall the visual and dramatic arts were not dealt with in a religious context. If true, that's a failing, because of course any form of compartmentalisation is contrary to Quaker belief in the sacramental quality of the whole of life. There's been a big change in recent years, which must be a good thing. I don't think even the most austere or unemotional Quakers ever suggested that intellect alone was sufficient for the spiritual quest. But if they never promised that religion would always make sense, at least it shouldn't make nonsense. There may be an impulse to believe in things which cannot be proved, but there is never an obligation to believe things which can actually be disproved. We accept the finite limits of our cognitive minds, and we accept that there are things beyond our present comprehension: but on matters which do lie within our comprehension we need not put up with incompatibility and contradiction, and if they seem to be there we must go to work on them with all our faculties, including the gift of reason. Quakerism has never asked me to give assent to anything which my reason tells me cannot be true. That is not always the case with other religions.

Maybe our habit of silence is an important safeguard. Maybe it helps us to avoid the trap of trying to put into words things which cannot be expressed in words? If there is any truth in that, does it follow that the Society should disregard demands, internal or external, for clear statements about our beliefs? Maybe.

NOTES

[1] John Robinson, 1963, *Honest to God*, SCM Press.
[2] Gerald Richards, 1978, reprinted in Quaker Forum 2001(5) as 'Quaker Theology – Trumps or No Trumps'. Gerald Richards states that early Friends were not Jesus-orientated: 'Fox preferred the Holy Spirit to the man'.
[3] W. Sargent, 1957, *Battle for the Mind*, Pan Books.

2

I HAVE TRIED TO describe Quakerism as I experienced it, growing up in the nineteen-thirties, -forties and -fifties. I believe it is recognisable by many of my contemporaries, but obviously my recollections will not tally exactly with everyone else's. It is an old joke that the question *"What does a Quaker believe?"* gets the response *"Which particular Quaker?"* Friends with different backgrounds will all have different recollections. My school contemporaries will have been differently influenced by the teaching to which we were exposed, and while for some people the beliefs absorbed in childhood, (whether less or more orthodox, scriptural, "liberal" or fundamentalist), have proved a satisfactory basis of faith ever since, others have moved on, reinterpreted, or rebelled. One of my family who was educated at a Quaker School in the 1980's told me that he felt Jesus was "rammed down their throats". He was thankful to sever all contact with Friends as soon as he left school.

If my recollections are correct Quakerism was a faith robust in practice if a bit vague in theology, satisfying intellectually if sometimes rather austere; taking as a text: *"In essentials Unity, in non-essentials Liberty, in all things Charity"* (printed on the front of every issue of The Friend for many years).

If that is right, Quakerism forty or fifty years ago was distinctly different from orthodox Christianity as promulgated by the mainstream churches. But that's no surprise – hadn't it always been? We all know about early Friends' refusal of oaths, "hat honour", and their public criticism of the religious establishment. But the arguments were not only about outward forms or social behaviour: they arose from conflicts of doctrine and belief, which were deadly serious matters in the climate of the time. Early Quakers had no doubt that they were Christian – indeed they were inclined to present themselves as the resurgent "true" Christians – but in the eyes of the orthodox they were dangerous dissidents. Quaker deviations from contemporary orthodoxy were greater than those of Luther or Calvin, or the much later disagreements which produced Methodism and the nonconformist denominations. If I am not mistaken (historians may correct me) the original Quakers were not just a peculiar side-chapel within a broad church: they were right outside it.

In our present age ecumenicism is highly valued, and inter-church co-operation is the order of the day. We seek common ground with other denominations and, up to a point, with other faiths. Many Friends find ecumenical collaboration enriching and enlightening, and they delight in our membership of CCBI. On that subject there has been much discussion. I am going to suggest that there are other, more important, relationships which Quakers could be developing. We should be looking outward, to other groups, different constituencies.

What groups? What constituencies? I am thinking mainly of people who profess no formal religion and repudiate all religious institutions. There are some among them, I believe, whose spiritual awareness (though they might not like that term) puts them close to the true spirit of Quakerism.

Who are those people? Many and various, but let's start with some near home – my neighbours, and probably yours too. They wear Greenpeace T-shirts or Amnesty ties, their cars carry FoE stickers, they abhor factory farming and seek organic products. Some would call themselves pacifists. Others wouldn't, but they still worry about Britain's part in the arms trade, and the legitimacy of armed intervention in Iraq, Kosovo or Afghanistan. They care about our treatment of refugees, and international debt, and the actions of the IMF and WTO. They are interested in ethical investment schemes, they may have heard of Triodos. We discuss all these matters with them. We discuss almost everything. But not religion.

Perhaps they are aware, these neighbours of ours, that we go to Meeting on Sunday. Maybe, casually, they wonder why. They may have heard about Quakers in the past, when they were questing teenagers, or students, or at a CND or Greenpeace demo. But it didn't catch on and, well, there are so many other things to do on Sunday mornings.

11

Can you blame them? What are their images of institutional religion, and of worship? What do they suppose is being offered?

Consider this statement: *God, the Creator of the world, who resides in a place called Heaven, sent his son Jesus to earth to preach a gospel of love and peace. However, Jesus's mission went beyond preaching. His task was to redeem mankind from the state of sin, into which we had fallen through Adam's and Eve's disobedience. By his willing acceptance of death on the cross Jesus bore the burden of all our sins, and thereby won salvation for us all.*

(No, sorry: a correction to that. Not for us all, only for those who believe in him).

That précis may seem unfair: but I think that until, say, the last 150 years, most people in Britain would have accepted it without much demur. Nowadays, for the vast majority of the population, it has no more validity than a fairy story.*

Consider the Creed which worshippers repeat at every Communion service: *"The only begotten Son of the Father... ..cruci-fied, dead and buried ....the third day he rose again... ...He sitteth at the right hand of God... ..and shall come to judge the quick and the dead...."*

Or consider the Catechism which Catholic children still learn by rote. Or consider the statement, repeated at almost every funeral, that the deceased has merely passed out of our sight to continue life on another plane, and we shall all meet again in due course on that plane. Such sentiments are supposed to give comfort to the bereaved. I wonder if they do? How many people actually believe them? Isn't it time we stopped pretending, and grew up?

Friends, we have a testimony of plain speaking. Why don't we stand up and say out loud, that the liturgy of orthodox mainstream Christianity is a litany of absurdities. The language may be beautiful, the imagery poetic, but much of the content makes no sense. These are fairy stories, myths, metaphors, parables, fables. To keep repeating outmoded mantras as if they were literally and factually true is an insult to intelligence. Most people in Britain realise this: that is why they have abandoned the church.

---

* Also no less validity. The best fairy stories embody symbolic truths.

More seriously, it is an insult to the underlying truths which the myths are intended to illuminate. For many, they no longer illuminate, they obfuscate and obstruct them.

To be fair, many people within the churches accept that the traditional statements should be taken as metaphor and myth. In clerical circles, discussions about the nature of God do not stick long at the level of *"Big Daddy above the sky"*. It is not only Don Cupitt and David Jenkins who are willing to use alternative images and newer expressions. Many other priests (probably most) do so in their private conversations. But as soon as they get back in the pulpit, all but the most radical preachers seem to feel obliged to revert to the old language, the old simplistic concepts. No doubt this is partly because they have to "go by the book " (of Common Prayer). But also, they sometimes say, it is because this is the language expected and recognised by "the man in the pew". But what about the person who is not in the pew – the one who no longer bothers to turn up?

Does this have any relevance to Quakers? I think so. Many Friends seem completely comfortable with traditional Quakerism (*or what they think is traditional Quakerism*), expressed in traditional language. Some of them get very uneasy when anything else is hinted at. From time to time one hears of seekers who have gone away from Meeting disappointed because the ambience was not as overtly "Christian" as they had expected. That is one side of the picture and it is sad. But on the other hand I wonder how many others give up for the opposite reason, because they cannot make sense of the Christian message in the way it is expressed. I believe that the "God-language" so dear to many, puts off many others. That is also sad: and I think it is important, possibly more important than our failure to attract Christians who have, after all, a choice of comfortable homes elsewhere.

I think that Christianity, as presented by the mainstream churches, includes a lot of off-putting nonsense. I think that a lot of Quakers would agree. So why are we so keen to get alongside those very same mainstream churches and play down our differences? What is stopping us from speaking out about the manifold absurdities, the emperor's clothes? George Fox wouldn't have held back. Are we just too polite? Are we slightly in awe of the ecclesiastical panoply? (Perish the thought!). Is it because those churchmen and women we get to know personally often turn out to be nice, sensible people with whom we have many basic values in common? One much-loved Friend who labours greatly in ecumenical endeavours has pointed out to me that working together has the advantage of avoiding duplication of effort as well as the opportunity of cross-fertilisation. I'm sure that is true at a personal level, but perhaps not at an institutional level.

Regarded dispassionately, some of the mannerisms of institutional religion are so bizarre as to defy parody. It is extremely easy to poke fun (remember Dave Allen). But I don't want to make cheap debating points. We all know people whose lives gain comfort and meaning and peace from their religious observances. Some of them are elderly, or lonely, or both: to ridicule them would be pointless and unkind. It seems that for many worshippers (not Christians only) the repetition of some familiar phrases and actions conveys a reality which is not entirely dependent on the meaning of the actual words: non-verbal messages akin, perhaps, to those which some find in music or dance. If that is so, though we may not wish to use those methods of worship ourselves, perhaps we feel constrained to be respectful of them. Also, perhaps some of us may have an uneasy suspicion that there might be issues we have not properly understood regarding ceremonial and ritual

Personally I have respect and affection for the Church of England. In the days of rampant Thatcherism, with the Labour Party in disarray, the churches at times seemed to be the only real political opposition. Their stances on poverty, inner-city deprivation, racism, and the immorality of monetarism, were points of light in a dark time.* I respect greatly the welfare work undertaken by the Salvation Army, or Christian Aid. And one remembers with humility the clerics who have spoken out boldly against Nazism and other tyrannies, and paid dearly for their courage.

Our local vicar is a tremendously busy man. He rushes round his far-flung parish with a smile for everyone, offering guidance to the young, cheer and companionship to the elderly, consolation to the distressed. Our community would be poorer without him. I like him and respect him, but that is despite, not because of, the things he says from his pulpit.

When treble voices are piping "Away in a Manger" around the Christmas tree I am as moist-eyed as any other grandfather. And

---

* eg. "Faith in the City".[1]

14

– on a very different level – the glory of the great cathedrals never loses its power to excite and inspire. I grew up in the shadow of York Minster, and will always be grateful to those who built it and maintain it. The devotion and commitment of the mediaeval crafts-men are breathtaking. (Let us not dwell on the wretchedly squalid conditions in which the builders lived and laboured, or think of other uses to which all that money and energy might have been put). I will travel willingly to view some mediaeval stained glass, or visit a Saxon church. When Bach's resounding *Sanctus* crashes out like a great bell tolling from an Abbey tower, I stand with the peas-ants in the fields as they pause, and cross themselves, and watch the monks file through the cloisters to keep their Offices: and I am aware that these are important threads in the tapestry of my cul-ture.

But – *and it is a very large "But"* – those experiences, though precious, are not primarily – to me – aspects of "Religion". They are aspects of Heritage. I wouldn't want to be without them, but they do not influence my moral and ethical beliefs, they do not show me how I ought to live my life or give me the strength to try. Well, perhaps that's not quite true, because after all inspiration is a function of all great art or great music. But that effect is not lim-ited to the overtly religious examples. A Schubert Mass ("sacred) is not necessarily more uplifting that a Schubert symphony ("sec-ular"). A classical Madonna may be very moving, but so may Rembrandt's or Hockney's portraits of their mothers: possibly even more so if we can approach them without suffering the imposition of an enforced reverence. Religion and Heritage are entangled, but they are not the same. We should try to disentangle them, difficult though that is.

In cynical moments, I wonder whether the authority of the church depends entirely on its external trappings and adornments. If the church were to discard all its robes and ceremonies, its odour of sanctity, the mystery and magic of ordination and ecclesiastical authority, and step down to meet its followers on level ground.....what would it become?

The same question can be addressed to the Monarchy. Was it Bagehot who advised the monarchy to maintain its mystique by keeping its distance? The monarchy seems set to disregard that advice, and it is discovering even now the consequences of embrac-ing the common touch.

And the church? If it discarded all its stage props, would there be nothing left but an empty theatre? Some would undoubtedly think so. I shall not go that far: I think there could be something left. It might even be a bit like Quakerism.

Bald cynicism is unhelpful. So can we agree that ceremonial trappings and archaic usages are at least, well, harmless? I have to say that I am no longer quite certain about that. My doubts are to do partly with those neighbours of ours if, as I think, they represent a multitude to whom religion (as presented by its institutions) is a turn-off. And alongside them I perceive many of my old school friends who are still trying to live by the values we learned together, but have given up going to Meeting and no longer describe themselves as Quakers or Christians. They have (in my view) thrown out the baby with the bathwater. That is not surprising, if the bathwater has become so murky or so cluttered with little plastic ducks, that one cannot see whether or not there is a baby there at all. My feeling is that as long as we persist in using the traditional language and imagery of Christianity we are cutting ourselves off from them, and from other groups and constituencies where we could be finding kindred spirits. And those constituencies are huge, compared to the pitiful and diminishing handfuls of active church members.

The only churches whose memberships are increasing at present are those on the charismatic or fundamentalist wings. The same observation can be made about Islam. It has been suggested that when secular humanism fails to meet people's needs, religious fundamentalism steps in to fill the vacuum. Then it may happen that authoritarian fundamentalism provokes, on the rebound, a backlash against all religion. One Friend recently referred to this as "a game of cosmic ping-pong" and asked: "Where do Quakers stand?"[2] A good question, made all the more timely by terrorist acts perpetrated in the name of religion.

If a new spirituality is to be found in places outside the religious institutions, where shall we look for it?

For a start, a growing number of people claim that spiritual truths are revealed to them by such practices as yoga, tai-chi, aikido, meditation, repetitive chanting, circle dancing, and so on. Not all devotees of these practices would feel comfortable with the word "spiritual", but they seem to be claiming benefits similar to those claimed by churchgoers, so we may think it a fair comparison.

Then there is also the growing army of people for whom the word "holistic" has become a talisman. They reject science and scientific medicine in favour of alternatives which, they claim, enhance not only their physical and mental health but also (some say) their spiritual well-being. Indeed, the concept of "holistic", properly understood, challenges the physical/mental/spiritual distinctions that have dominated western science and theology since Descartes.

Matthew? "Popularity of poems"

I don't feel compelled to argue with all those people. I am willing to be impressed by their testimonies – but on one condition. I want to see evidence that their activities produce some benefit, in the form of greater wisdom, or insight, or kindliness, energy, serenity, or *something* (please, *anything!*) which enhances their lives and, through them, the lives of others. In my experience that is sometimes true but not always. (You may ask: should we issue the same challenge to regular churchgoers, or meeting-goers. My answer is: Yes, we should.)

Church-goer or Cinema-goer?

The peace movement has burgeoned in recent decades. The passion and commitment of earlier generations of pacifists is strengthened by newcomers bringing scientific rigour and professionalism, enabling Peace Studies to develop as a respectable academic discipline and a coherent ideology. Much credit for that belongs to the Quakers who started the School of Peace Studies at Bradford University. Others who are adding their weight to the arguments include members of health-care professions through such bodies as International Physicians for Prevention of Nuclear War, and Medicins sans Frontieres. At least one learned journal* includes articles on mediation, non-violent direct involvement in conflict, or the psychopathology of aggression, alongside factual reports on weapons or landmine injuries. This must be a hopeful sign.

To take another example, some very strange ideas are to be found in the writings of modern scientists in the fields of cosmology and particle physics. For most of us the concepts pass right over our heads, because they defy common-sense, and the mathematical arguments are incomprehensible to us. If the whole universe came into existence with the "Big Bang", what was there before? We are told that the question is meaningless, as time itself

---

* *Medicine, Conflict and Survival* (publ: Frank Cass, London).

17

did not exist before that. Our concept of space/time is challenged, and with it goes temporal sequentiality, and the familiar notions of cause-and-effect. It is as if the idea of eternity – in the sense of being outside the confines of sequential time – is no longer a purely theological or metaphysical notion. How does that affect the idea of Creation as an historical act? T.S. Eliot wrestled with this in several poems.*

Some writers say that the world revealed by modern physics bears rather striking resemblances to the world-view of Buddhist and Taoist mystics.[3] Be that as it may, it does seem that the traditional scientific tools of analysis and synthesis (which are not being abandoned – nor should they be) are leading us into unfamiliar areas where those very tools are seen to be inadequate, and different modes of thought, no less rigorous, but different, are called for. Heraclitean rather than Pythagorean, say those who understand such things.

In the past science and religion were often presented as mutually hostile.** If scientific thinking can begin to accommodate concepts beyond sequential logic, and if religion can discard some of its obscurantism, perhaps a reconciliation will be possible. Not a moment too soon, if it will stop mankind vandalising the earth.

Which brings us to another group of people, those who are willing to spend dangerous and uncomfortable days and nights in trees or underground tunnels, or being abused or manhandled because they feel strongly about ecology, nuclear disarmament, animal welfare, or some other cause. And also those whose disgust with our greedy and destructive society leads them to turn their backs on it altogether, becoming "New Age Travellers" or something similar. And the greater number who have modified their lifestyles somewhat out of concern for the environment. There are, of course, many religious believers who are fully committed to social and political reforms: Donald Soper and Bruce Kent come immediately to mind. But I am more concerned here with the greater number of unbelievers.

---

* eg. *The Waste Land* and *Four Quartets*.
** But Quakerism has been able to accommodate many scientists including some very eminent ones in our own time like Arthur Eddington and Kathleen Lonsdale, both of whom declared that they felt no conflict between their religious beliefs and their scientific knowledge.

In each of those groups (of course they overlap) there are people – I would claim – whose philosophical or ideological base puts them closely alongside Quakerism.

But hold on a minute. Let us not rush to embrace with equal fervour all the activities and ideologies of these groups. They do not all have equal validity, and some will not withstand close scrutiny. Personally I would not claim close kinship with the Animal Liberationists who resort to deadly violence, or most of the people who claim spiritual enrichment from taking drugs. Especially at the start of a new millennium we can be sure of an upsurge of superstitious nonsense – occultism, clairvoyance, pagan rituals, ley lines, little green men from space, feng shui, and the whole gamut of tawdry tabloid trash. As Chesterton put it:- *"when men cease to believe in Something, they won't believe in Nothing, they will believe in Anything"*.

Aha! So having demonstrated that orthodox religion contains a lot of absurd nonsense, now we admit that New Age Spirituality (an umbrella term I use here loosely and shall not define) is also full of it. So what is the point of abandoning one kind of daftness merely to embrace something equally daft?

A valid objection if it were what I am proposing, but it is not. What I am suggesting is that Quakerism is particularly well-placed to straddle several worlds, appreciate the truths in each and reject the dross, and build bridges. I think we could do this because as a Society we have some very important strengths, ideological and practical. If those strengths were utilised more widely the effects could be very great indeed. Perhaps not as earth-shaking as the preaching of George Fox in his day, because times and attitudes have changed: but Quakerism could be again, as it was then, a very important seminal influence in the world, well beyond its own present boundaries.

A bold claim indeed! Is it justified? Read on.

NOTES
[1] *Faith in the City*, 1985, Christian Action (précis edition).
[2] Billy Frugal, 1998, in *Earthquaker: Newsletter of Quaker Green Concern*, Issue 22, Spring 1998.
[3] Capra, Fritjof, 1975, *The Tao of Physics: an exploration of the parallels between modern physics and Eastern mysticism*, Fontana Paperbacks.

3

QUAKERISM WAS BORN in the mid-17th century at a time of intense religious and political ferment. Quakers were just one group among many dissenting sects – Ranters, Shakers, Anabaptists, Muggletonians, Fifth Monarchy Men and others. Most did not survive, and nowadays only specialist historians can remember what they all stood for. Quakerism, however, did survive. It became, for a time, the third largest religious group in the land, a real challenge to the Anglican and Presbyterian establishments, a power to be taken seriously by the politicians of the day. Later when the initial fire was damped down, and the banners of evangelism passed to Wesley and others, the Quakers survived, and even in their so-called "quietist" period they prospered, and were respected.

Why? Did Quakers have a greater vision, a more sublime wisdom, a clearer message, than the other Dissenters? Were they (are they) the elect of God? I think the answer is more prosaic. George Fox was certainly an impressive preacher, his ministry was powerful, prophetic, and in tune with the aspirations of the times, and his courage was awe-inspiring; and among his associates were other men and women of towering moral stature – those whom Ernest Taylor named the "Valiant Sixty".

But Fox's genius had another aspect which is not often emphasised but was, I believe, very important. He was a superb organiser. The guidelines and procedures that he laid down, the whole shape of the organisation he founded, were remarkable, and remarkably efficient. Its principles were firmly based and clear, and also broad – sufficiently broad for the Society's administrative structure to remain serviceable and virtually unchanged right up to the twentieth century. Very little modification has been found necessary, and in 350 years there has been relatively little schism or internecine strife. We should cherish those original principles, and refrain from any gratuitous meddling with the practices which arise from them. They are a gift to us from the past, a gift we should value in our own time.

But didn't I say earlier that Quakerism in the 21st century needs to change? The inconsistency is resolvable if we can distinguish between those Quaker attributes which are fundamental and those which are secondary. *"In essentials Unity, in non-essentials Liberty."* But which is which? A good place to start would be *Quaker Faith and Practice,* which somehow contrives to be both contemporary and timeless. Here I want to mention just a few issues which I believe to be particularly relevant in Britain today.

First, the basic Quaker tenet that light should be accepted from whatever source it comes. Religious insights, wisdom and guidance are not restricted to the Gospels, not even to the whole body of Christian teaching, or the texts of all faiths, but above all they are found in the living experience of each individual. That was Fox's radical message and he meant it to apply not only at the level of spiritual revelation, but also in more mundane matters. Each person, young, old, educated or uneducated, "worthy Friend" or young newcomer, has access to truth – or perhaps we should say, to aspects of truth. We recall that the early Quakers called them-selves "Friends of Truth". We relish the idea that spiritual insights come to each person experientially. We remind each other of Fox's challenge: "Christ saith this, and Paul saith that: but what canst *thou* say?" My truth may not be identical with your truth, but nonetheless it is mine, and for me it is a truth.

In this context we are not talking high theology only, but also very practical and specific items of everyday behaviour. So, you may think, this is a doctrine of extreme individualism, a do-it-your-self system of faith and ethics which must surely be a recipe for chaos, and a very insecure foundation for a group identity? Yes, there's a problem, let's admit it. But there are some checks and bal-ances which, properly applied, lessen the tension.

If we expect our individual insights to be respected, the con-verse must be a willingness to treat other people's insights seriously, to listen to them carefully, and to expect to learn from them. Thus a Quaker, confronted by an opinion or a practice which he or she finds alien or unacceptable, will not (should not) respond with instant contradiction and counterargument, but will try (should

21

try) to discover why the other person holds that view, and see if there is common ground on which to build.

It was in that spirit that the American Quaker John Woolman set off in 1762 to the Susquehanna:

"....to spend some time with the Indians, that I might feel and understand their life and the spirit they live in, if haply I might receive some instruction from them, or they might be in any degree helped forward by my following the leadings of truth among them".[1]

The Quakers of New Jersey had long been more sympathetic than most white settlers to the native American tribes, but the situation was still dangerous. John Woolman's family had reason to be concerned for his safety, and it is evident from his Journal that Woolman himself recognised, and accepted, a serious risk of capture and death. But in the event he emerged unscathed having established mutual understanding and respect, and surely that was due to his humility and sincerity, his willingness *"to receive some instruction from them".* (It has taken most of us 200 years to realise that the "Red Indians", generally stigmatised as savages, did indeed have some valuable instruction to offer, notably about man's relationship with the natural environment.)

A second fundamental Quaker tenet is summarised in the phrase *"that of God in every man"* which means, among other things, that no-one can be written off as irrevocably wicked (people will say "not even Hitler" – or perhaps now Osama bin Laden). It stands in contrast to the credal *"..miserable sinners.....no health in us"* and underpins our peace testimony and our opposition to capital punishment.

Let us next consider some aspects of Quaker decision-making, which may seem trivial but are, I believe, fundamental. The conduct of Friends' administrative meetings is based on the premise that, for every issue under consideration, there is a right or best outcome, and we all want to find it. Some will refer to this as seeking the Will of God in the matter. though nowadays that phrase does not come easily to every Friend's lips, and indeed it may seem unnecessarily pretentious if we are discussing, for example, what colour to paint the Meeting House walls or whether to install a gas boiler. But whether the issue be profound or seemingly mundane, the underlying belief is that the right way forward will become apparent if we listen to each other attentively and patiently, seeking whatever is true and useful in each other's statements and dealing kindly with whatever is erroneous. A story is told (and I'm sure it is true) of a Preparative Meeting in Cambridge at which the question of a carpet for the meeting room floor was under consideration. Different views were expressed, and eventually Anna Bidder rose and declared: *"I'm sure God doesn't care at all what decision we make about the carpet. But I'm sure He cares a great deal how we make that decision"*.

Our business meetings are really meetings for worship within which administrative matters are considered. Decision-making in those circumstances can be very cumbersome. because there should be no final decision as long as any Friends present are still expressing opposing views – if "we are not in unity". So, voting would not be appropriate. One consequence of that is that there should be no outvoted minority left feeling disgruntled.

That is the theory. It doesn't always work in practice and sometimes it fails catastrophically, but the wonder is that actually it does work quite well, quite often. Of course there are occasions when an individual may be unhappy about a conclusion that the meeting as a whole is about to accept. Then it is up to him or her either to stand firm and continue the search for agreement, or to say to him- or her-self that the wisdom of the group is probably greater than that of any individual ("even me"). This process of seeking unity rather than voting has been applied in some non-Quaker settings. In negotiations about disarmament, for example, it is painfully obvious that a majority decision simply won't do, because if any of the parties, even just one and however small, goes away feeling oppressed and disgruntled, a treaty or agreement simply will not work. We need only think of Palestine or Ulster. And it is surely no coincidence that Quakers have often found useful roles as mediators in such conflicts.

Another idiosyncratic process in Friends' administrative meetings, is the practice of composing a Minute in the meeting as each item is dealt with, recording the agreement there and then (or if no agreement is reached, recording that fact). This apparently minor detail is in fact rather important. Once made, the Minute is "owned" by the meeting. Anyone with experience of committee meetings under non-Quaker auspices will surely see the significance of that. The current buzz-word is "transparency".

23

Still on the level of practical procedures, let us consider the process whereby a Friend who feels strongly about an issue (in Quaker-speak, a Friend with a Concern) can take it to their local meeting to be discussed and tested. The issue might be a personal one – something the Friend in question feels he or she ought to do, or not do. Or it might be a cause that he or she thinks the Society of Friends, or the wider society in general, ought to support. In the past it may have been expressed as: *"God is telling me to do this"*, but nowadays probably not.

Local Friends, who know the person well as a neighbour and regular member of the worshipping group, will set aside time to listen carefully to the concern which is being expressed, and try to evaluate whatever course of action is proposed. From this patient and sympathetic discussion various outcomes may emerge.

The group may say: *"Yes! We accept that what you are feeling and intending is genuine and important for you. Go ahead – you have our loving support. Come back to us if you need any help"*.

Many a Friend has embarked on a course of action buoyed up by the awareness of sympathetic support from his or her home meeting.

Or the group may say: *"Yes! We share your conviction! You have identified a genuine and important issue and we will join with you in acting on it. Henceforth this is not only your concern, it is our concern as well."*

For example: the support given by Yorkshire General Meeting in 1792 to William Tuke for the foundation of The Retreat to pioneer the humane treatment of mental illness: mirrored in our own time by Friends' concern for Community Care.

On the other hand the group may say: *"No. We think you have got this thing a bit out of proportion. Your proposed course of action is, we fear, unlikely to achieve the ends you are seeking. What seems to you to be a leading of the holy spirit is, we think, open to more mundane interpretations. We think you ought to think it through more fully."*

To which they might (should) add a rider: *"Will you let us (or some of us, or one of us) try to help you in the process of thinking it through?"*

These examples demonstrate how the beliefs and behaviour of an individual may be moulded and modified by the group: and that is one reason why such an apparently individual-centred system

24

does not lead inevitably to chaos. The important point is that the modifying influence is not Holy Writ, or tradition, or instructions handed down by an "authority": it is the thoughtful personal attention of fellow-members, neighbours who know each other and care about each other.

Obviously there are some situations where the wisdom and understanding deployed by the local group are insufficient; and in that case help is sought by bringing in Friends from a wider field or with specialist knowledge. Their motivation and mode of working will be the same. Inevitably there are some occasions when an individual, intensely motivated, does not accept the guidance of the group, and feels irreconcilably at odds with it, and perhaps with the Society in general. No-one, and no system, is perfect. People resign their membership, sometimes in high dudgeon and for reasons that an observer may consider insufficient. But those sad failures do not negate the value of the process: indeed the observer sometimes feels that the breach might have been avoided if the procedures had been followed more carefully.

If the Friend's concern is about something with general consequences, after being accepted at local level it will be passed through appropriate channels to be considered by widening bodies of Friends, until eventually it may become accepted as a concern of the whole Society. And at every stage of the process the originator of the concern should be able to present it and carry it forward. They might not always choose to do so, but the opportunity should be there. Nowadays that is sometimes neglected but I believe the principle is very important. The initiating Friend should never be told: *"This is now out of your hands – you must leave it to people further up the hierarchy"*. Friends with experience of political manoeuvrings in the non-Quaker world will surely recognise the radical nature, and the value, of that practice. The modern buzzword is "empowerment". In a world where people often feel disempowered and are bitter about it, the difference is crucial.

From these examples (there could be others) it is clear that the Society of Friends in Britain is what a management consultant would call a "Bottom Up" rather than a "Top Down" organisation: and that is, I think the kernel of George Fox's administrative genius, and a major factor in the survival of the Society through the centuries. Ideas, concerns, proposals and projects start from the periphery: there is no central authoritarian hierarchy. The same principle applies to membership. An attender wishing to join does not apply to a national office, he or she is admitted by a local Monthly Meeting, and that happens after what our management expert would probably call a Peer Evaluation conducted at local level.

No hierarchy? That was the theory (despite the original charismatic leadership of George Fox); and for most of our history it was also the practice. Recently some Friends have sensed some erosion of that principle, with the growth of central and specialist committees at Friends House, and what is sometimes called a "Friends House Bureaucracy". The tendency may be exaggerated (I think it is), but if it is the case that some "ordinary Friends" at the periphery are feeling disempowered, even slightly, that is a challenge to our traditions and an issue we should address.

But there is something else in Quakerism which helps to protect us from hierarchical tendencies should they occur (in addition, that is, to the inherent stroppiness of members). At every level in the Society the Elders, Clerks, and members of committees are not appointed as "Officers" but as "Servants of the Meeting". "*Servants*" is a significant word not, I think, an empty one. Friends do not seek personal power within the Society: they do not promote themselves or stand for election. In fact I suspect that any Friend who thrusts him- or her- self forward for a position of power or influence will be regarded as disqualified for that very reason. There is a shrewd and deep-seated belief that power should only be entrusted for a limited period, and preferably to a person who would really prefer not to have it at all.

That emphasis on service is not limited to roles within the Society. It sits very close to the centre of the Quaker ethos. In fact it is what the outside world knows about us. Some years ago my wife and I travelled in eastern Europe in the company of a senior Lutheran priest, who went to meet local congregations, and we went with him. In one group we were invited to say something about Quakerism. To most of those present the word Quaker meant nothing: but two elderly ladies nodded, and said to our companion "Ah, der Kvakeren! We remember. They came to help us after the war when we were starving. We never knew they were religious". (Note: they didn't just send money or parcels: "*they came*". That was remembered).

In the far west of Ireland there is (I have heard) an old Quaker burial ground. For many years there have been no Friends living anywhere near, but the little plot stays tidy and cared-for. A visitor who remarked on this was told: "The Quakers were the people who helped us at the time of the famine, when no-one else did." I have heard similar stories from the Welsh mining valleys.

That tradition of relief work is still being carried on today in trouble-spots throughout the world. When Robin Cook visited Russia as Foreign Secretary in 1998 he spent some time with Chris Hunter, a young Friend in his twenties from Yorkshire who was organising relief and reconstruction work in Chechnya. The Foreign Secretary went away impressed and personally recommended Chris for recognition in the New Years Honours.

A few years ago Friends in Belfast opened a charity shop. They had an unexpected visitor: Mo Mowlem, then Secretary of State for Northern Ireland. She made time in a busy schedule to go and be photographed at the shop by the press, because (she said) she so much admired the quiet painstaking work of peace-building which the Quakers had carried out over many years.

Service is what the world associates with Quakers: it is a badge we wear. It influences the careers that young Friends choose for themselves, and the commitments that individuals undertake in their communities or more widely. Perhaps it partly explains why our membership contains disproportionate numbers of teachers, doctors, social workers and others in the "public services", and relatively few business magnates or self-made millionaires. Maybe it was in the mind of my colleague, an elderly Scotswoman, who said *"I never knew you were a Quaker, but – och, I always thought there was something nice about you!"* And the lady who kept a sweetshop in York, who told me when I called after many years that she could usually differentiate Bootham old scholars from those of other York schools.

Above all, the ideal of service is exemplified most vividly by the young Friends of my generation and earlier who rcgistered in wartime as conscientious objectors and saw front-line service in the Friends Ambulance Unit or some other non-combatant unit. They were not running away from danger. They were saying, in effect: "I am willing to die. I am not willing to kill.". A different interpretation of *"dulce et decorum est pro patria mori"* to the usual one, but no less idealistic or courageous.

In this chapter I have listed just a few of the things that Quakers do. The list is a melange of principle and practice, some items rather grand and others that may seem banal. I have not tried to separate or prioritise them because they feel to be inextricably interconnected.

Perhaps we can add one more attribute. Remember the story of Neave Brayshaw and the ticket collector?* It was that same unbending honesty and unshakeable integrity which characterised early Friends and got them into so much trouble. (The same integrity also helped them to withstand the persecution it provoked.) That obsessive attention to detail which led John Woolman to dress entirely in unbleached linen because cotton-growing and the dyeing industry were connected with slavery. The honesty which led observers in the eighteenth century to remark with astonishment that "you may send a small child to the Quaker's shop", knowing it would not be cheated: a reputation that led directly to the establishment of Quaker banks and businesses. Perhaps even today we can include integrity in our list of Quaker attributes: I hope so.

Are these things no longer needed in the 21st century? Or are they needed more than ever?

What about accepting the light from wherever it may come? Is that relevant or not in a multicultural society, and wherever people are seeking ethical guidelines in a post-Christian culture?

What about treating seriously the insights of others, avoiding confrontation and seeking common ground? What about decision-making based on transparency, a search for unity and empowerment rather than majority dominance?

What about being able to rely on a like-minded and loving group or network when one needs support or guidance in bad times – or good ones for that matter? What about a sense of belonging?

What about service? In a self-centred society where materialism and self-indulgence are trumpeted by advertisers and cloaked in glamour, where the rich get obscenely richer and market forces rule and even the so-called Public Utilities seem to care more for their shareholders than their customers? Is anyone out there still

---

* (See page 2).

interested in choosing a job or lifestyle which puts back more than it takes out? Has Margaret Thatcher's dreadful remark that "there is no such thing as society" really penetrated to the depths of our culture? Is altruism dead and buried? I don't believe it is; but are we proclaiming that belief in our words and actions? And are we actively seeking allies?

What about our Peace Testimony? Terrorist actions in September 2001 opened the eyes of many people who never thought of themselves as pacifists to the realisation that violence cannot be controlled by violence alone. Mediation and peace-building are on the agendas of governments as never before, but there is much high-level confusion.

And what about integrity? We have come to expect sleaze as a fact of life and not only in politics. In sport, in business, in service industries public or private, we are bombarded by evidence of cut corners and shoddy deals. Does nobody care any more about doing a job properly, the way it should be done, even if it's not cost-effective, or short-term profitable, or a vote-winner at the next election? Are all journalists unscrupulous? Must spin always take precedence over substance? Does everyone falsify their expense accounts and their tax returns? Does anyone who receives too much change, give it back? Does anyone who finds a wallet hand it in? The meticulous, pernickety, obsessional attention to detail which characterised the financial dealings of our Quaker forebears would now seem quaintly old-fashioned to many. Do Quakers still aspire to those standards? I hope so. Does anyone else? Yes, I'm sure of it: and while they may be a minority they are not negligible, and they are not all Quakers – yet. And that, of course, is one of the points I have been trying to make all along.

I suspect that by now orthodox Friends – if they have stayed with me so far – will be feeling restless. A whole chapter listing the characteristics of Friends but hardly a mention of God, or Christ, or faith, or worship! Surely all those procedures and attitudes are mere epiphenomena on the surface of something deeper? After all, we are supposed to be the *Religious* Society of Friends – are we not? Hasn't the cart somehow got round in front of the horse?

NOTES
[1] *John Woolman's Journal*, Whittier's edition, 1871.

29

4

A FEW YEARS AGO Ben Pink Dandelion, who is a very thoughtful Friend, and a tutor at Woodbrooke, remarked that if certain trends continued there would soon be nothing left of Quakerism except *"Friends' way of doing things"*. That seemed to him to be a dismal prospect.

I told him I couldn't share his gloom. I think there is a lot to admire in Friends' ways of doing things. But the next question is – do they only work when there is an overt spiritual basis and consensus, or will they stand on their own merits, without dependence on religious beliefs? Most Friends will probably think a spiritual basis is essential, and maybe it is. But what makes Quakers recognisable has more to do with our behaviour than our beliefs. It is our actions, our way of life, the things we stand for (and things we won't stand for), that identify us in the eyes of the world. Those are what people remember about Quakers, and what we remember about those who influenced us in our formative years.

Of course I know what my friend Ben was getting at. Is there something that underlies all those Quaker "ways of doing things". I hope there is, because if not, if we behave by custom and habit alone, we could get stuck forever in the *status quo*. We would have no compass to steer by when facing new situations – and there are plenty of those in our current world (genetic modification is a good example). It's just that the way the underlying "something" is usually expressed is, I think, outdated. The familiar idiom is keeping out people who ought to be welcomed in.

Here is an assessment by a non-Quaker historian:

"The finer essence of George Fox's queer teaching, common to the excited revivalists who were his first disciples, and to the "quiet" Friends of later times, was surely this – that Christian qualities matter much more than Christian dogmas. No Church or sect had ever

made that its living rule before. To maintain the Christian quality in the world of business and domestic life, and to maintain it without pretension or hypocrisy, was the great achievement of these extraordinary people. England may well be proud of having produced and perpetuated them. The Puritan pot had boiled over, with much heat and fury; when it had cooled and been poured away, this precious sediment was left at the bottom".[1]

Thank you, Professor Trevelyan, you are very kind – embarrassingly so. In essence, then: "by their fruits ye shall know them" – OK? Yes, but fruits don't just appear from nowhere, they grow on trees. For 350 years we've taken it for granted that our tree is Christianity. Trevelyan makes that assumption. If we seriously want to get alongside people who are put off by Christianity, to function effectively in a post-Christian world, we'll have to do better than that. And it won't be enough just to find new words to express old meanings, if there are actually new meanings to explore as well. Don Cupitt leads the way here.[2] His opinion of Quakers is almost as flattering as Trevelyan's, and it puzzles me that Quakers do not seem eager to reciprocate.

Back to basics. What's really essentially distinctive about Quakers?

Well, they go to Meeting for Worship on Sunday mornings. Actually, not all of them do: I know several who don't, but are still Quakers in my estimation, even if not in their own.

What is Meeting for Worship all about? That question has been addressed by many wiser people than me, from Thomas Kelly[3] to George Gorman.[4] I don't feel competent to tackle it. All I can offer is some disconnected personal observations.

I have sometimes thought that at the end of a Meeting, Friends rather resemble an audience leaving a concert hall after a musical recital. One notices the same stretching of muscles, mental as well as physical, the same sense of coming back to earth, with tacit agreement that something worthwhile has been satisfactorily completed. Of course there is one obvious difference: no applause. That is because there is no distinction between audience and performers; we were all involved. (Quakers didn't abolish the priesthood – in case you needed reminding – they abolished the laity.)

31

Smiles are passed around, while the Clerk reads out the notices that bring us back to everyday practicalities. As Friends stand up and start to leave the room a few words may be exchanged about the ministry (or the music), as if to confirm that an experience has been shared, and it was in some sense a valid one, (or perhaps not). Not many words though, because the experience cannot be captured in words, it may easily be distorted, and that too is recognised. A dispassionate critique might come later, if at all. Just now, as we all make our way towards coffee and sociability, the music, the silence, is still with us. Was it grandiloquent Verdi today, or provocative Mahler, delicately intricate Chopin or rumbustuous Gershwin? There are so many different kinds of enrichment in the concert hall, and in the Meeting House.

Let's not exaggerate. Not every Meeting for Worship is a powerful experience. When we are held by the silent music we feel it and are grateful, but we do not expect to feel it for the whole hour every Sunday. For that matter I don't suppose each churchgoer comes away from every Communion or Mass overwhelmed by the Transcendental Mystery of the Body and Blood of Christ. Not every meal is a banquet. Sometimes a Meeting that for one person is intensely moving has little or no impact on the person sitting adjacent. But there are other occasions when the whole gathering seems to be feeling and experiencing something together, in unity. Those are the unforgettable Meetings. They are what we call a "Gathered Meeting".

My first experience of that was as a teenager, in an open-air meeting on the summit of Firbank Fell in Cumbria. A coachload of Bootham boys and Mount girls were taken for a few days to visit places famous in Quaker history around Lancaster, Swarthmore Hall, Brigflatts and Pendle Hill. We were led by that wonderful teacher, Elfrida Foulds, and she had the story-telling skill to bring people and events of 1652 to life before our eyes. We took it all in with adolescent seriousness which was not at all solemn, and a very deep feeling of companionship.

We strode with youthful energy up the slope of Firbank Fell, and we sat in a silent circle on the ground, beneath the stone outcrop from which George Fox had addressed a multitude, the birthplace of Quakerism marked on the map to this day as Fox's Pulpit.

It was a perfect setting for something wondrous to happen, and we were ready and waiting.

What I remember is the quality of the silence, and the feeling of rightness, of being a part of something rich and meaningful. There was some spoken ministry but I don't recall its content. I don't think I felt the "Presence of God" – certainly not as any kind of hovering supernatural Being. It was the coming together, the submerging of individuality in a sort of connectedness, in a gathering enfolded in friendship. And then that connectedness seemed to spread more widely and deeply until it encompassed – what? – how? – momentarily, perhaps, the whole universe – and beyond.

Such experiences are almost impossible to describe. Words like "numinous" and "transcendental" don't carry the meaning. Maybe the Taoist concept of The Way is helpful.

I think that among British Friends today the most significant division is not between so-called Universalist and Christocentric tendencies,* but between those who have experienced the reality of a gathered meeting and those who have not, or have forgotten it. I found that expressed compellingly by Christine Trevett in her 1997 Swarthmore Lecture[5] though her terminology, and maybe some of her beliefs, do not coincide exactly with mine. Gathered meetings are not predictable, and they cannot be created to order. External circumstances and surroundings may play a part, as they did that day on Firbank Fell, but there are no essential prerequisites. It can happen in a large meeting or a small one, in a grand Meeting House or someone's front room, among friends or relative strangers.

The experience has a particular quality in that it does not feel like "*something that we are doing*", but rather "*something that is happening to us*". I suppose that is what leads people who are so inclined to engage in supernatural speculations, and prompts the word "mystical". We could have lengthy discussions about words. We might want to ask each other what the concept of "worship" can mean to a person who does not perceive God as an external Being. Such discussions are only slightly helpful. Undoubtedly some worshippers feel the presence of an unseen "other" with whom they have a personal relationship, perhaps even a dialogue.

---

* See *Quaker Faith & Practice* (1955) 27.04.

Others don't. We need not argue about it and we must not. From George Fox onward, Quakers have emphasised the importance of the *experience*, not the thicket of words that spring up like weeds to surround and conceal it.

If the gathered meeting is so significant, does that mean that any meeting which does not reach those depths is, for the particular individual, a failure and a waste of time? Not necessarily. Let us not underestimate the satisfaction and – yes, the enjoyment – of sitting quietly for an hour with familiar and like-minded friends, feeling a "belongingness" with the place and the people, drawing some sustenance from the spoken ministry of others (even if selectively), trying to empty ones mind of its usual clutter of ephemera (even if not quite successfully). In meetings with no spoken ministry, and even in those which do not reach the depths, there is communication in the silence. I don't want to call it telepathy because that has the wrong associations, it's just a word and it doesn't explain anything. But most of us can remember occasions when the thoughts and feelings circulating in one's own mind were suddenly put into words by another Friend, seemingly "out of the blue" and sometimes in surprisingly precise detail. Those who have not experienced the phenomenon are entitled to be sceptical, but to the regular meeting-goer it is almost commonplace.

If I were challenged to "explain" such experiences, I would have to rely on imagery and metaphor. You can try this one, if you like:

> You are in an aeroplane flying over the sea, and you pass over an archipelago of islands. Each individual patch of green-brown seems to float separately on the blue surface. Boats ply between them, lighthouses and radio masts send messages from one to another, there is evidence of interaction: but each island is a separate entity within its own shoreline.

> Now take an atlas that includes cross-sections of the earth's crust. It shows (as of course you knew) that these islands are not separate, they are the protruding peaks of an underwater mountain range. However deep the troughs, it would be possible (at least in theory) to link one island with another without crossing the sea, by tunnelling under the sea bed. Taking a larger view, each underwater mountain range is not a separate mass, but part of the underlying crust of the planet, linked to every other part, if only one could tunnel deeply enough.

John Donne said it long ago. As human beings we seem to be separate entities but we are not. Enclosed within the shoreline of each ego, our usual conscious way of relating with each other is by messages that we send across the channels between us. (Some of the channels are narrow and easily crossed: others are wide and deep, and some contain violent tide-races dangerous to negotiate). But under the surface each one is part of a continent, and each continent is attached to every other one, and ultimately to the universal ground of being of every living thing.

The metaphor is a close relative of Carl Jung's concept of the collective unconscious. Is it possible that in the right circumstances human beings can communicate with each other at a deeper level, below the surface of consciousness? Such communication would not be mediated by words – (words belong to the surface world of the conscious mind) – and it might not always be lucid or coherent, but we feel it to be profound – and the word *profound* is apt.

Is it possible, even, that when we penetrate deeply the depths of our own beings, and then go still more deeply into levels which lie beneath individual separateness, we might start to become somehow "in touch" with the universal ground of all our beings – with the universality of life itself?

Does that explain the experience of the Gathered Meeting?

No, it doesn't. It doesn't "explain" anything at all. It's only a metaphor. Don't fall into that trap. It's an image, a metaphor, a way of looking at things, not intrinsically better than any other imagery (but not necessarily worse). If you wanted to give a name to the *Universal Ground of all our Beings,* I suppose you could choose to call it "God". But it's probably better not to do that, except when talking to such as Paul Tillich, John Robinson or Don Cupitt, because generally speaking I'm afraid it'll only cause confusion.

If Meeting for Worship is so important and central to Quakerism, can a person be a Quaker who does not go to Meeting regularly – or at all? Most Friends would probably say: No. I don't know. To live up to high standards of behaviour by self-determination alone, responding to one's own personal light, making one's own moral and ethical decisions unaided by an external moral authority – that is never an easy path to tread. Few of us, if any, are strong enough: we need help. Quakers find help in the shared experience of Meeting for Worship and the fellowship which stems from it. Other people, obviously, seek it elsewhere, and who am I to say they do not find it?

We were asking whether some Quaker processes and practices might be adopted by people who live outside Quakerism and eschew everything that has a religious smell about it. So we come back to the questions: to what extent do those practices depend on attitudes which derive from shared values, and to what extent do those values depend on our underlying belief-systems and how do those relate to our chosen form of worship?

For example, I suggested earlier that in making collective decisions, Quakers act as if for every issue there is a right or best outcome, and we all want to find it, believing that the right way will become apparent if we listen to each other attentively and patiently, seeking whatever is true and useful in each other's statements and dealing kindly with whatever is erroneous. That is a rather noble aspiration. Let's admit frankly that Friends themselves don't always live up to it. Is it realistic to expect it of a group whose members are not so closely bound by strong spiritual ties? Probably not. But the alternatives – the way things are usually settled in the world at present – are not working very well. The world needs very urgently to find better ways. I am not supposing that everyone out there is waiting to seize Quaker methods with avidity. I had in mind some people, some groups, who are our kindred spirits already. I do not think our kinship, or potential kinship, should depend entirely on shared Meetings for Worship. And let's not be conceited, we are not the only group that sets high standards and whose members are bound together by strong ties.

If we believe that Quakers have something particular to offer, and we want to offer it more widely, we should take steps to discover those kindred spirits and get together with them. We shall need to cultivate a common language, never forgetting John Woolman's principle *"that haply I might receive some instruction from them"*. We may join them, or attract them to join us.

The first option (us joining them) happens a lot already. Quakers are numerous in the ranks of CND, FoE, Greenpeace, CAAT, Drop the Debt, Refugee Aid, Community Relations and so on. Many of the lobbies and campaigns and protest movements of the last quarter-century have been initiated or supported by Quakers. In the Peace Movements especially it is fair to say that Quakers have enhanced the effectiveness of the organisations. But is that due to Quakers as individuals, or Quakerism as an ethos or set of principles or practices? The Meetings for Worship outside the gates of Greenham or Menwith Hill stand out as rather rare exceptions.*

At some point we have to acknowledge a particular difference between Quakerism past and present. Time was, before CND, Greenpeace and all those other groups existed, when any Friend's concern about social or political issues was expressed through the Society. John Bright was a distinguished Parliamentarian, but a Quaker first and foremost. William Tuke or Elizabeth Fry would naturally use their Monthly Meetings as the channel through which to test and further their concerns, for it was the most effective channel available. Nowadays things are different. Whatever concern may come upon you, you are quite likely to find that there is already a group in existence, outside the Society of Friends, devoted to that very issue. You may well feel that such a group is where you should make your contribution, and if you ask local Friends they will probably agree.

But there is a price to be paid. Throwing yourself with enthusiasm into this other lobby or action group, you will now have less time to give to purely Quaker business, less time to attend Monthly or General or Yearly Meetings. You may also begin – dare I say it? – to have less inclination. If you support the new cause financially you may have to cut down your contributions to Friends' work, so your involvement with this concern may not strengthen and stimulate your local meeting, or the Society of Friends in general, as would have been the case with William Tuke or Elizabeth Fry. On the contrary, it may in some measure weaken it, as we all fly about busily in all directions.

What about the second option (them joining us)? That is partly a matter of making our presence better known and more accessible in our localities. A lot of outreach work of that kind goes on all the time, it is important and it has its successes. But new members

---

* For a recent example see Rachel Milling's report: *"There were some Quakers there .... because of their involvement with other organisations .... It would have been good to have had a meeting for worship .... if we had known. Many of the young people had never heard of [Quakers] .... At the meeting house [they were] heard wondering about this funny place which wasn't a church but seemed to be religious"*.[6]

are not being recruited as fast as old members are dying off, and we know what that must mean in the long run.

I am proposing something more radical. I think we should recognise that we live in a post-Christian culture, it not only surrounds us but we are part of it. To be effective in that culture we must change the way we think and talk about ourselves. Alex Wildwood recognised that in his Swarthmore Lecture[7] where he announced himself (bravely I thought) to be a post-Christian, but I have not noticed many Friends following his lead. If we are to attract a wider range of people, with whom we have some things, but not necessarily everything, in common, it may mean dropping the "Religious" label, and the language that goes with it. That may be a price we have to pay. It would not be the only price, and we must ask seriously whether we are really ready to go down that road.

NOTES

1 Trevelyan, G.M., 1944, *English Social History*. Reissued by The Reprint Society, London (Longmans Green), 1948, pp269-70.
2 Cupitt Don, 1994, *The Sea of Faith*, SCM Press.
3 Thomas Kelly, 1944, *The reality of the Spiritual World* (and) *The Gathered Meeting*. Reprinted by Quaker Home Service Committee, 1996.
4 George Gorman, 1973, *The amazing fact of Quaker Worship*, Quaker Home Service Committee.
5 Christine Trevett, *Previous Convictions* (Swarthmore Lecture 1997), Quaker Home Service.
6 Rachel Milling, "Blockading Faslane", *The Friend*, 9 March 2001.
7 Alex Wildwood, *A faith to call our own* (Swarthmore Lecture 1999), Quaker Home Service.

5

THE AMERICAN QUAKER John Woolman was a prime mover in the campaign to abolish slavery, and in 1772 he decided that to advance that cause he should visit England. A transatlantic voyage in those days was a major undertaking, made even harder for John Woolman because he would not travel on any boat implicated in any way with the slave trade, and he declined the financial support offered by Friends that would have purchased him some relative comfort. Eventually he found a boat that satisfied his conscience and set off, travelling steerage, clutching a Travelling Minute from his own meeting to Friends in Britain.

By that time English Friends had put behind them the rebelliousness of earlier years. They were now respectable members of society, honest, conscientious, prosperous, not given to social protest or contentious political activism, and with a horror of the excesses of evangelical "enthusiasm" displayed by followers of Wesley and Whitefield. The Meeting of Ministers and Elders that met as a preliminary to the Yearly Meeting in June 1772 was a particularly solemn, august and impressive body – *"parliament itself perhaps could hardly offer a more solidly well-to-do group"* * This sober gathering had been sitting for less than an hour when in stepped John Woolman, straight off the boat. We are told that:

> *"Coming in hastily and unannounced, the stranger Friend, just out of the vessel's steerage quarters, with a correspondingly dishevelled toilet, which was itself peculiar in its undyed homespun and grey-white beaver hat, naturally created some apprehension"*

Some apprehension indeed! The consternation was intense as Woolman strode up to the Clerk's table to present his credentials.

---

* I have based the description of this event on the accounts given by Rufus Jones[1] and Janet Whitney.[2]

39

The Travelling Minute was read out. It commended John Woolman "as one in good esteem among us" (he was actually one of the most highly regarded Friends of his time in all America), and recommended him to the "Christian care" of English Friends.

The assembly received this with barely-concealed dismay. The prospect of this weird Yankee, with his odd appearance and bizarre dress, being at large in their country was intolerable. As an authenticated Quaker, travelling in the ministry (an official designation) he would bring their beloved Society into disrepute! The silent hostility was palpable. At length a weighty Friend rose to his feet. He was, I think, Dr. John Fothergill, a member of a notable Yorkshire family, later to be the founder of Ackworth School. Choosing his words carefully he suggested that the visitor could now feel that the Concern that had been laid upon him was discharged, and he should feel free to return to his own country. Quiet, polite, and Quakerish in tone, no doubt, but the meaning was crystal clear, the snub unmistakable.

Such a humiliating public rejection of a certificated visitor, his mission not even heard, was unprecedented, yet it seems likely that John Fothergill had expressed accurately the feeling of the meeting.

John Woolman was visibly shattered and sat with tears streaming down his cheeks. The meeting waited in silence. They may have expected an unseemly outburst or an ignominious retreat: but neither happened. Eventually Woolman rose to speak, and he did so briefly and with dignity. He said that he could not feel himself released from his duty, but since Friends were not in unity with him he would make no claims on them, save only that he was skilled in a certain trade, and if any Friend cared to put him in the way of a little work by which to support himself, he would be grateful.

He sat down, and a long silence ensued, and during that silence something happened. It can be like that sometimes in a Quaker meeting: a change as subtle and barely-perceptible as a change in the direction of the wind or a modulation of key in a piece of music. No words spoken, but a different atmosphere developing, the *sense of the meeting* (that elusive concept) swinging round to a new direction. The hostility to Woolman slowly melted, thawed by his quiet sincerity.

He sensed the change, and in due course felt free to stand and speak again. This time he spoke fluently and at length about the evils of slavery and his concern to end it. John Woolman was a masterful speaker, and the Ministers and Elders recognised his spirit and power, and were moved. A chastened John Fothergill acknowledged his error and humbly begged John Woolman's pardon. The concern was accepted, the Travelling Minute endorsed, and the campaign against slavery was supported.*

The point of this historical digression is simply this: suppose that next year's Yearly Meeting (or MfS, or your Monthly Meeting) were interrupted by the arrival of a political activist or so-called "eco-warrior" such as the roads protest campaigner who gained some fame in the 1990's by the name of Swampy. Hairy and none-too-clean, his clothes stained by tunnelling underground or tattered by treetop living, speaking with passion and wanting an immediate response – wouldn't he seem as outlandish, embarrassing and out-of-place as John Woolman seemed in Gracechurch Street in 1772? Wouldn't Friends recoil in confusion and dismay? Wouldn't they (that's you and me) protest about the "right ordering" of Quaker business? Wouldn't Swampy be snubbed as Woolman was snubbed?

I am sorry to say that I think he would be. If so, the prospect is shameful. Middle-class respectability is a potent influence now as it was in the 18th century. But, to be fair, it is not the whole story, and the reasons might not be all despicable. There may sometimes be genuine and deeply-felt apprehension about courses of action which are undertaken, or proposed, by people outside the Society or, for that matter, inside it. Such apprehensions are not always relieved by discussion or explanation. A current example is the use of force against weapons of mass destruction by Ploughshares supporters; is that a kind of violence? Is it a good end but a bad means to it? Friends are divided.

We must not sweep such issues under the carpet. We have to consider them carefully and discuss them thoroughly, and avoid being hijacked by our (or someone else's) emotions. We might

---

* During the ensuing months Woolman won wide respect among English Friends. Tragically he contracted smallpox and died later the same year at the age of 52 in York, and he is buried there.

41

legitimately ask Swampy to give us time to think, to gather evidence, perhaps to seek specialist advice.

But if we try to deal with such matters by debate and discussion alone we shall be guilty of disregarding at least one of the Quaker principles noted earlier and omitting at least one of the Quaker procedures. It was not through discussion that John Fothergill and the other Elders changed their response to John Woolman. They did not weigh evidence and then decide to give him a hearing. They allowed themselves to be impressed by his sincerity, and they sat quietly, for as long as necessary, in the discipline of a meeting for worship, until they could sense what might lie behind the unfamiliar presentation, and respond to humility with humility.

We cannot be sure that a latter-day Swampy, snubbed in one of our meetings, would be able to match John Woolman's dignity of response. Very few people indeed can do that. Our responsibility is therefore all the greater. But it seems that our business meetings, from Preparative Meeting to Yearly Meeting, are often so busy nowadays that the agendas leave little time for that kind of quiet reflection and waiting. Oh dear! How can we think of persuading other people to use our Quaker methods if we do not use them properly ourselves?

If Swampy or one of his successors came not to Monthly Meeting but burst in on us during a local Meeting for Worship on Sunday morning, would we be better disposed to discern and respond to his concern, since on those occasions we have no preconceived agenda.

Possibly so, and I hope so. But I think we must acknowledge that here might be a different obstacle. Many Friends are engaged through the week in responsible and demanding jobs. Some of them deal constantly with difficult situations or awkward people, and for many their working lives are punctuated by crises. At the same time they may be having to juggle with family commitments, and still find time to support some good cause or charity. By Sunday they are – in the modern phrase – "stressed out". I am thinking particularly of Friends who are young and vigorous. Many older Friends are relaxing in retirement after leading just such stress-filled working lives themselves.

For such Friends, Meeting on Sunday morning can be a haven, an opportunity to re-charge the mental and spiritual batteries, to feel secure and relax in the company of Friends who are also friends. Rightly or wrongly they do not go to Meeting to be challenged or upset. Wrongly, you may think, and I suppose that's true – though the reasons are understandable enough. They do not want to feel got at. It's bad enough when the blissful silence is broken by a Friend whose well-intentioned words are badly out of tune with ones own thoughts. And we've all suffered from the speakers whose too-frequent and overconfident ministry mistakes their personal preoccupations for a divine message. The last things one wants are the jangle of off-key guitars (metaphorical or actual). or the axe-grinding of an enthusiastic proselytiser challenging one's taken-for-granted beliefs. No, can't we keep that sort of thing for a study group, or refer it to a committee? If we're being asked to support some immediate action, could we hear about it, please, with the rest of the notices after meeting, not during it? In the meantime, as John Fothergill isn't with us today, would someone gently lead the stranger out and explain to him kindly that Friends don't ....?

So are we really ready to take the risks of issuing a more general invitation? Or would we rather remain as a cosy group of peculiar people, with a reputation for good works and upright living unsullied by dispute or contention? If we were to widen our appeal by dropping some bits of our historical baggage, (while rediscovering some other bits), Quakerism might change the world, but we must not expect it to remain unchanged itself. In fact we have noted that the process of modification is already happening. The question is, are the directions in which we are moving the best ones?

It is a fact that in this century the majority of Friends in Britain were not born into Quakerism, nor brought up to it from an early age. They have come into it in adult life. It's very good to have them with us, of course it is. Without them the Society would be tiny. They include many of our most active and energetic members. I certainly don't want to upset them, I wouldn't dare! But among those who have come from Anglican, Methodist or other traditions there seem to be some who, despite having left home, want to cling on to bits they valued in what they left behind. That's entirely natural and unsurprising, but it can mean that their faith, and the way they express it, is at best a *melange,* at worst a confused muddle, of

Quakerism and mainstream Christianity. I would guess that for some of those people the earlier chapters of this booklet may have contained some surprises.

I wonder whether these Friends are the same ones who rejoice in our ecumenical links, our membership of CCBI and local Councils of Churches? I have no way of knowing that – but it would not be altogether surprising if it were so. I would not presume to criticise them for it, nor would I criticise those who maintain dual membership between Quakerism and one of the mainstream churches (though that is a position I find difficult to understand).

I have been saying all along that we should spread ourselves by getting more closely alongside other people with whom we have things in common – if not necessarily everything. I suggested at the end of chapter two that "bridge building" might be the mission to which Friends in the 21st century are called, and I claimed that we are particularly well qualified for it by our history, our basic values, and some of our organisational practices. Accepting light from whatever directions it may come, we should be able to relate to a wide range of people. We should not be put off by those who express their spiritual or moral values in terms which are less "orthodox" or "religious" than the terms we use, or not "religious" at all.

So, you may say, by the same token we should surely be prepared to extend bridge-building also in the direction of the mainstream churches, not being put off if they express spiritual or moral values in terms which are *more* "orthodox or religious" than the ones we use. The point is valid. So, roll on the ecumenical bandwagon?

Yes, but… we should always be careful that any alignment we have with a particular group or viewpoint does not cut us off from others that we value. That is the catch, and that, with regard to orthodox Christianity and the mainstream churches, is where my doubts begin.

I have proposed that we should look around for people with whom we may find kinship, and I have already indicated some places where we might find them. Are there any guidelines?

First and most obvious, we should have some values in common, even in a post-Christian world, (perhaps especially in a post-Christian world). There are some people who act as if the

44

trouble we manage to accommodate members who are neo-Catholic, Neo-Buddhist, neo-atheist, neo-almost anything. Some regard that as a weakness. I see it as a strength. So my plea to those Friends who wish us to be allied more closely to the mainstream churches is: do not claim exclusiveness, do not even use words which seem to imply exclusiveness. Think of all those other people out there, the ones who have turned their backs on religion and will turn their backs on you too if they perceive you to be tarred with the same brush.

And the same applies to anyone who claims exclusive access to ultimate truth through other activities, whether by meditation, chanting, or drug-taking, or any variety of "new age" activity. In my experience the devotees of some of those practices can be just as blinkered as the most ardent Christian.

My third guideline or *caveat* refers to what I have described previously (perhaps rather rudely) as absurdity or nonsense. This is a particularly difficult area because what seems ridiculous to one person may be very precious to another. I have claimed that the Quakerism with which I grew up never asked me to give assent to anything that my reason told me could not be true. Quaker beliefs and practices may not always make perfect sense, but at least they don't make nonsense. Idiosyncratic and odd, perhaps, but internally consistent and – in a sense, I think – "reasonable".

Of course reason alone is inadequate. Reasoning is only one of our mental functions and not always the most important. Spiritual growth, interpersonal relationships and moral judgements cannot be tied down to narrowly rational thought processes. But does that mean that when we enter an area labelled "religion" we should leave all our critical faculties outside and abandon reason altogether? I think not. I think that is a road towards bigotry and fanaticism.

For some people religion would be incomplete without miraculous or inexplicable happenings. Some seem to regard them as a test of faith. Perhaps the *frisson* of fascination they produce is an echo of childhood nights when goblins, ghosts, and God himself lurked indiscriminately behind the bedroom curtains; or perhaps they are images from deep in the race unconscious, like methane bubbles rising to the surface from the bottom of a stagnant pond.

I don't think we need be po-faced about wizardry, but I don't believe it has much relevance to mature spirituality.

I hope we shall avoid identifying ourselves closely with any groups whose beliefs are heavily invested with magic. In our spiritual journey, when we come to a place where reason alone is inadequate, (as we surely will), let us acknowledge the mystery openly. But let us try to avoid expressing it in words that are tarnished by superstition and that create unnecessary barriers between people.

For Quakerism to fulfil its potential as an important influence on 21st century attitudes and behaviour, we must turn away deliberately from all kinds of obscurantism, and build on our assets of simplicity, clarity, straightforwardness, and consistency. It is a task which will require all our powers of discernment, a lot of sturdy common sense, and consistent use of the checks and balances which our organisational structure provides.

We are at a crossroads, Friends.

Aren't we always?

There is a main road that seems to lead towards the City of Christian Unity. The tarmac looks smooth, though there are certainly potholes round the next bend. If we choose to travel that road we can be in respectable company. The bishop is keen to give us a lift, and his ancient Daimler is elegant and comfortable, despite a loss of power on the hills and a few rattles under the bonnet. Alternatively, we can choose to go skipping along gaily with the scooters of the Tambourine and Hallelujah Brigade.

Or we could strike off in a different direction, following one or other of the motley crews who seem to be travelling hopefully towards a destination still shrouded in mist. We might catch them up. We might overtake them. Who knows, we might be able to give them a sense of direction, we might even find ourselves leading them. Conceivably, we might end up in territory not too far from the bishop, after all.

Alternatively, we could carry on strolling down the little lane that is Quakerism, enjoying the peace and quiet, pleased if a few strangers choose to come along with us as long as they don't make too much noise. Or we might remain huddled under our umbrellas at the roadside in the rain, trying to decipher the faded words on an old signpost, peering rather pathetically at an out-of-date map.

47

Or shall we stop worrying about what we believe, or what anyone else in or outside the Society believes? Should we simply conclude that navel-gazing and *angst* will not get us anywhere? Is it enough to concentrate on what Quakers have always been best at, which is getting down to it and doing things – and doing them our way? Or is that a cop-out?

The choices are yours.

NOTES
1 Rufus M. Jones, *The Quakers in the American Colonies*, London, Macmillan & Co., 1923, pp405-6.
2 Janet Whitney, *John Woolman, Quaker*, London, Harrap, 1943, pp370-1.

Additional Bibliography

Various authors in:

Harvey Gillman & Alastair Heron (Eds), *Searching the Depths: Essays on being a Quaker today.*

Home Service, 1996, *Who we are: Questions of Quaker Identity*, Booklets A & B.

Quaker Resources for Learning: QHS & Woodbrooke, 1995.